Santa Catalina. If ever an island were created that could please everyone, this would be it. Avalon, calm and serene, is a haven for yachting enthusiasts and visitors alike. All in all, Catalina has something for everyone's taste.

SANTA CATALINA ISLAND

THE STORY BEHIND THE SCENERY®

by Terrence D. Martin

Terry Martin, a graduate of the University of California with a degree in biological sciences, was the Naturalist for the Catalina Conservancy from 1983 to 1989.

We wish to thank Misty Gay, Naturalist and head of the Catalina Conservancy Department of Conservation and Education, for updating the factual material for this printing.

Jeff Gnass's photography provided most of the scenic views for this book. Like all visitors, he was enthralled to find the natural beauty of Catalina in virtually its original state.

Located less than 20 miles off the southern California coast, Santa Catalina welcomes visitors with a picturesque coastline, ample anchorages, clear water, and fresh air. Those who venture into the interior find primitive and rugged backcountry with magnificent vistas of the surrounding Channel Islands and of the mainland coast.

Edited by Mary L. Van Camp. Book design by K. C. DenDooven.

Fourth Printing, 1998

Friendly, protected coves and inviting hills symbolize Catalina's appeal to visitors.

Few places on earth are loved by so many people for such different reasons as Santa Catalina Island, known simply as Catalina to locals. Nowhere else can you find the pleasures of beach community living delicately balanced with remarkably unspoiled wilderness.

Avalon, Catalina's center of population, is a world-renowned beach resort town noted for its climate, ocean sports, businesses, and friendly charm. But the rest of the island is famous too, as a place where you can experience the moods of nature unexploited, of California as it was hundreds of years ago.

Easily accessible by sea and air and only 20 miles offshore from Los Angeles, Catalina appears much as did all of California before modern civilization covered the land. The island's wild hills and steep cliffs remain little changed from the way they were the day Cabrillo discovered them. And preserved today in the rugged slopes and deep valleys are remnants of a flora even older than history. Santa Catalina is a natural and recreational treasure, most of it maintained in a primitive state— a living reminder of California's natural heritage.

The Pervasive Sea

Most everyone enjoys Santa Catalina, but few understand what makes it so special. To a keen observer, a few minutes of quietly reflecting about the surroundings makes the answer clear. Hear the sound of surf crashing, see the sparkling blue Pacific, smell the clean salt spray, feel the cool sea breeze: the restless ocean is the single most important factor responsible for the island's unique character.

The sea has interacted with the monumental forces of geology to create this isolated and magnificently rugged chunk of earth. The Pacific has acted as both a barrier and a highway to various living things, inviting colonization by some while denying access to others. The Mediterranean climate of cool, moist winters and warm, dry summers that makes southern California so desirable is significantly altered at Catalina. Here the temperature and moisture-moderating influence of the sea yield warmer winters and cooler, moister summers. In turn these climatic factors affect all island life.

Rock-Rending Birth

The steep, cobbled beaches of Catalina's southwest shore are both enchanting and intriguing. Thundering breakers roll boulders as if they were beach balls along the base of 1,500-foot cliffs of tortured lava and twisted metamorphic rocks. What formed this impressive seascape? The story is written on a confused jigsaw puzzle of rock that has yet to be fully deciphered. Attempts to reconstruct the geologic history reveal that forces responsible for shaping the island accompanied the birth and death of a segment of the earth's crust.

Eons ago many of the rocks that make up the island were part of the sea floor. This material rested on the basement rocks of the slow-moving Farallon plate, a relatively small block of the

Quartz sheets forced between layers of metamorphic material gives Ribbon Rock its distinctive appearance. Here lies the record of 120 million years of geological history. Each year dozens of geologists trek the hills and puzzle over the rock outcrops for clues to understand the processes that formed them.

WILLIAM W. BUSHING

earth's crust. The Farallon plate gradually slid eastward, carrying material toward the continental plate of North America. Where the two plates joined about 119 million years ago, a slow-motion collision occurred beneath the sea's surface. It was a big collision: basalt crumbled; other rocks bent like taffy; and the North American plate rose as the Farallon plate was driven underneath it by the Pacific plate—a process known as *subduction.*

Sediments and basalt fragments, scraped from the advancing Farallon plate, accumulated on the hanging wall of the continent or were carried as much as 20 miles beneath the earth's surface. The resulting heat and pressure changed the very structure of the rocks, transforming some sediments to schists and bending layers into bizarre shapes. The debris scraped off by the collision formed the embryonic island of Catalina while the melted material jammed beneath the continent helped lift up the Sierra Nevada.

Approximately 20 million years ago a new material was added to Catalina's metamorphic base when the last of the Farallon plate was subducted beneath the North American plate. For 5 million years igneous rock blanketed and even squeezed its way into the older rocks of Catalina, and a volcanic archipelago arose off the California coast. This volcanic and hydrothermal activity left a legacy of mineral wealth including silver, lead, and zinc.

Late in the Miocene Epoch (between 23.7 and 5.3 million years ago) the shallow basin where Catalina was born was transformed by extentional and wrench faulting. In this process the block on which Catalina rests was moved about 156 miles north from its previous location near the Mexican border and rotated 60 degrees clockwise to reach its present position off southern California. In addition, the island was subjected to vertical movement and changes in sea level, changes that are still occurring.

Thus, Catalina was once larger than it is now. A mile or more seaward from the present shore and 80 feet beneath the sea lies a vast, wave-cut terrace with valleys once cut by streams. This terrace is the remains of an ancient shoreline. Further uplift and downdrop, along with changes in sea level, have altered the island's size at various times. At Little Harbor Point on the island's south side, uplifted sections that were once beaches are now wave-cut terraces hundreds of feet above the present shore.

The scars of the island's violent birth are borne beautifully. Jagged volcanic peaks dominate the skyline while metamorphic rocks, some bent in fantastic ribbon shapes, comprise much of the island's southwest side. The beauty of these

rocks has not gone unnoticed, for many face stones on early twentieth-century Los Angeles buildings came from Catalina. The material for many of the rock walls in Avalon came from the East End and Empire quarries.

Even today the island's face is constantly changing. Erosion battles with the rocks, slowly wearing them down. Sometimes, sudden but violent slips or floods occur, drastically altering the landscape.

AN ISLAND IS MORE THAN ROCK

From the air Catalina is a 21-mile-long ridge of mountains extending from northwest to southeast and varying from half a mile to 8 miles wide. Its total area is almost 75 square miles, with 54

While most people think of geological forces as imperceptible, this fresh landslide at Ripper's Cove gives ample evidence of such forces at work. Catalina's recent history is one of geological uplift, as evidenced by vertical cliffs at the sea's edge around much of the island. But forces of erosion are constantly trying to wear the island down to sea level.

From the air you can appreciate Catalina's unique qualities. Isolated by the sea from many effects of human change, the island is a craggy monument to the way California used to be. The sea influences all aspects of island life. Cool and calm in summer, in winter it is blasted by occasional storms. These factors affect the island's climate, making the vegetation almost like a part of northern California anchored off Los Angeles.

miles of coastline. From above you can appreciate its isolation; 25 miles separate Catalina from the nearest of the other Channel Islands. Imagine the effect of such isolation. Think what it took for life to get there and how few organisms could make such a trip.

Some plant seeds arrived on air currents, buoyed by structures like parachutes. Others arrived by sea, sprouting on the shores, or perhaps landing with the remains of a tree trunk or of a tangled mass of roots—a mass scientists call a raft. Many species arrived at the island with animals; birds probably brought seeds from blackberries and from the hollylike *toyon*. Man also brought many plants to Catalina, including the oats that dominate the grasslands, and accidental baggage like the hitchhiking star thistles. But fewer species have managed to become established on Catalina than on the mainland. Only some 400 of the thousands of California native plants are found here, evidence of the effective barrier formed by the sea.

The plants that did arrive on the island found a unique environment. Catalina's summer coastal fog makes the 12 inches of average annual rainfall go farther than on the nearby mainland, while the ocean's nearly constant temperature serves to moderate the winters. In concert with climate, the island's rugged topography includes a vast array of slopes, exposures and elevations, and resulting microclimates. These provide diverse ecological niches for four prevalent and several minor plant communities; less rugged relief would support fewer types.

Plant communities—associations of plants that share similar requirements and grow together—are different at Catalina from their mainland counterparts. Island plant communities tend to have a parklike appearance, due in part to the effects of grazing goats. The structure of these communities is different because some prevalent mainland plants just never made it to the island. Even plant species that occur in both places are sometimes different in appearance, environmental requirements, and genetic structure.

JEFF GNASS

An ancient wave-cut terrace overlooks Shark Cove at Little Harbor. Rocks and boulders, eroded out of the landslide slope, like chocolate chips washed from cookie batter, dot the beach. Extending seaward from this site is an underwater canyon many feet below the present sea level. When this canyon was cut by stream erosion, the sea level was much lower and the island much larger.

The plants of Catalina's ecosystem are special, but they are changing in response to variations in climate, introductions of animals and plants, extinctions of native species, and conservation efforts. The island offers visitors an opportunity to appreciate these special plants as well as to gain insight into how ecosystems evolve and function.

Santa Catalina is special for its diversity. A six-mile walk carries you from a coastal desert to moist oak woodland. On the exposed headlands near the westernmost part of the island is maritime desert scrub. This is a special association of plants adapted to the surprisingly intense drying effect of prevailing ocean breezes combined with the harsh afternoon sun.

The MARITIME DESERT SCRUB community is composed of cacti and other drought-adapted plants common in arid Baja California. The *Bergerocactus*, or velvet cactus, has fine, hairlike spines which reflect the sun and create shade while they also protect the plant from being eaten. The needlelike spines of the cholla (CHOY-yah) cactus are very different. They protect the plant, but also serve to spread new chollas by anchoring to fur, boots, or anything else that moves too close. By the time the unwanted hitchhiker is removed, it is far from its parent plant and ready to start a new clump of cholla.

Rain brings this desert community to life. With moisture the showy yellow and magenta flowers of the cacti sprinkle color even on harsh hillsides. The summer ripening of the prickly pear fruit is a taste treat for people as well as for many animal residents including ravens and foxes. Widespread throughout the island, this cactus is frequently cursed by hikers for its spines, but it has preserved rare plant species from extinction by acting as a natural barbed-wire enclosure for seedlings.

Uphill from the desert scrub lies a major shallow-soil community aptly named COASTAL SAGE SCRUB. This low-growing gray-green association of sages and other plants is found predominantly on south-facing slopes near the sea. This community varies in appearance depending on its exposure to sun, wind, and salt spray. The characteristic low gray version found on the Pacific side of the island is composed predominantly of white sage and California sagebrush. These species are responsible for growth, form, and color as well as the distinctive pungent aroma of this community. On the island's channel side, different species including Saint Catherine's lace add variety in size and color to this community.

The association of the bush sunflower with the prickly pear cactus is a unique aspect of the plants on the island's west slope. In several instances such plants serve to identify and protect the shell-laden kitchen-midden sites of former Indian inhabitants.

This broad expanse of prickly pear, cholla, and velvet cactus above Indian Head Rock attests to the harsh dryness created by westerly winds, sun on the south slopes, and salt spray.

Wildflowers like these goldfields carpet island grassland when early grass growth is slow and late seasonal rain prevails.

JEFF GNASS

WILLIAM W. BUSHING

JEFF GNASS

While walking through these scrubby coastal plants, you might pause to indulge your senses. The distinctive fragrance of sage alerts you that the community is appropriately called coastal sage scrub. Grazing pressure of past herds of domestic animals has thinned the vegetation in some places, so mostly inedible species like white sage dominate, giving this community its distinctive appearance.

Coastal grasslands once stripped by goats have been rejuvenated by restoration projects. Near Salta Verde Point, this landscape of clumps of bunch grasses is reminiscent of California before the introduction of European annual grasses. Preservation and restoration help conserve valuable resources so that future generations will be able to appreciate them in their natural state. The distant, isolated cobble beaches offer protection to animals once common on the mainland, including abalones and harbor seals.

Where slope and soil conditions permit, a GRASSLAND community exists. Moist grasslands produce an abundance of wildflowers in winter and spring. Slopes on the channel side of the island frequently greet winter boating enthusiasts with displays of goldfields and owl's clover. Although the wildflowers have not changed much since man's arrival, the grasslands were quite different. Vast acreages were covered by native perennial bunch grasses, lending a tufted, pale-green appearance to the hills year-round. But introduced graz-

With winter come the snowy white flowers of island ceanothus in the chaparral plant community on the slopes near Avalon. Common near the east end of the island, chaparral looks like a miniature forest of small trees and shrubs. While shrubs dominate this community now, an alternate community of wildflowers awaits the next beneficial fire that will bring new life and color to this area.

DOUG PROPST

JEFF GNASS

Wild apple, found on the mainland only on the Palos Verdes Peninsula, illustrates how different Catalina's plant associations can be from most of their mainland counterparts.

ing animals devoured the native grasses. As a result, most island grasslands now comprise introduced grasses that are golden brown in summer.

The native grasses dominate only in poor soils. Hope is not lost, however. Reduced grazing pressure, the efforts of conservationists, and the competitiveness of the hardy bunch grasses have already resulted in an increased abundance of this beautiful native plant.

Over the ridges to the north side of the island, on the east- and west-facing slopes of stream drainages, appears the ubiquitous southern California CHAPARRAL community. The island version of this community is distinctly different. Common mainland plants are missing, their places filled by relicts of a moister mainland era, including the stately tree-lilac, the wild apple, and the rarest small tree in California, the Catalina mahogany, known from

only a few naturally occurring individuals in a single canyon.

Much of the chaparral on Catalina is unusual. Many shrubs are umbrella-shaped, as if pruned by a gardener, the result of grazing by goats in times past. The yellow color of the hills around Avalon in the spring is due to the introduced shrub called French broom. This has replaced the native vegetation that once covered the hills with the blues of lilacs and the whites of greasewood. The balmy climate supports virtually all Mediterranean-type plants, so almost any introduction of a plant from such a climate thrives here. Some come from South Africa and Australia, others from South America and the Mediterranean itself.

Chaparral on Catalina is much more open than on the mainland, in part because of the different species making up the community, but also

Oaks on Catalina are frequently complex hybrids, a botanist's nightmare of confused characteristics but an artist's paradise of wind-contorted shapes and sizes.

because of at least 150 years of grazing. Grazing by goats and rooting by pigs probably also account for the low incidence of fires on the island. Fire, contrary to what some people think, is important in keeping chaparral healthy. Without fire, some plants grow decrepit and die, and nutrients are not recycled.

Many chaparral plants are adapted to fire. Some have seeds that need to be heated before they germinate. Certain trees sprout back when they are burned, rejuvenated in the process. Recent small fires have shown that many species of rare island plants in unburned chaparral spring up everywhere after a fire. As long as grazing by goats and pigs interferes with the island ecosystem, however, fire must be denied its role.

WOODLAND communities flourish on Catalina in places with rich soil and abundant moisture. North-facing slopes and deep, protected canyons are generally forested. But within the constraints of slope and moisture is a wide variation in forest types: the riparian (streamside) woodland of cottonwoods and willows looks different from hillside oak woodlands, and dense groves of Catalina ironwood and cherry have their own distinctive appearance.

Oak forests on the island are different from those along the coast. Coast live oak, dominant on the mainland, is absent, having missed its chance for arrival in the sweepstakes of dispersal. The oaks that do grow on Catalina are special, however. Majestic island oaks grace favored hillsides with a beauty not found on the mainland nor usually on other islands. In addition, unusual hybrid oaks lend variety in structure as well as size to the forests, while flowers and ferns weave a delicate springtime carpet in undisturbed areas.

Island plants, adapted to the cool, moist, northern California-like climate of the island's north slopes, often have larger leaves and more treelike

One of the island's largest trees is the Catalina cherry. Unfortunately for those who would harvest the cherry's fruit, it is mostly pit with only a small amount of tasty pulp.

statures than their mainland relatives. A good example of this is the Catalina cherry, a large relative of the mainland's holly-leafed cherry. A truly unique forest of these trees is found in Cherry Cove, named for one of the biggest groves of Catalina cherries. This forest of 30- to 50-foot specimens forms a pure stand. These trees, with their waxy green leaves, produce large quantities of fruit in summer. The cherries, once gathered by the Indians, are now harvested by the birds. The Catalina cherry grows naturally only on some of the Channel Islands and in San Julio Canyon of the Sierra de la Giganta of Baja California.

The Catalina ironwood, a rare, stately tree, is probably the most interesting tree on the island. Small groves of this shaggy-barked, dense-wooded, tall and slender tree are found only in the cool, moist valley bottoms and north-facing slopes. They are living relics of forests that have not existed on the mainland for millions of years. Such trees are reminders of a cooler, moister mainland climate. The ironwood subspecies of Catalina is found nowhere else on earth, while its relatives are found only on the other Channel Islands.

The Catalina ironwood has come close to extinction. Few seedlings are found in nature and fewer still survive, mute testament to climatic changes and the effects of feral grazing animals. Fortunately, a few groves of this beautiful tree are protected, and reforestation plans are being enacted.

On north-facing coastal bluffs there thrives a variety of coastal sage scrub little affected by the ravages of grazing animals. This is the COASTAL BLUFF COMMUNITY, held immune by its inaccessibility. It exists where coastal fog and sea cliff meet, forming a distinctive environment populated by unusual plant life. Because of its immunity to grazing, this area boasts the highest proportion of

Saint Catherine's lace is found only on Saint Catherine's Island: Santa Catalina. Truly a giant among the buckwheats, this plant often grows to a height of ten feet. The beauty of the flowers and foliage, coupled with the plant's low water requirement, have made this species attractive to southern California gardeners.

oy—

National Parks

e Culture of
Native Americans

hose who then
nt to know more
a complete series of books

RY BEHIND THE SCENERY ®

Conservancy offer hope
that this beautiful relict
will be with us for
generations to come.

JEFF GNASS

JEFF GNASS

endemic plant species on the island. Saint Catherine's lace flourishes here but is found nowhere else in the world at the subspecies level. This plant is characterized by its white, lacy head of flowers in summer and its rusty-red crown in winter.

The coastal bluffs provide a haven for species of stonecrops and dusty millers that are found only on the California Channel Islands. Yachting enthusiasts who have visited this island for years are amazed to learn what rare and special plants grow on familiar cliffs. For them, such plant life adds a new dimension to the cliffs' beauty.

Much of the plant life of Catalina Island is special, rare, and of biological importance. Although many types that grow here are also found on the other Channel Islands, eight exist only on Catalina itself. More than ten percent of the native flora is very rare, having not been recently observed or collected. If this resource on Catalina were not protected, we would lose its beauty, a glimpse of the past, and a chance to understand how ecosystems and evolutionary processes operate.

TERRY MARTIN

The island oak is found only on the Channel Islands.

DAVID WEISSMAN

Generations of natural selection have resulted in a new cricketlike species uniquely adapted to island life.

The aquatic garter snake probably arrived by "rafting" on a downed tree from an ancestral population in Santa Barbara County.

The malva rosa, a channel islands' endemic. Grazing once reduced this species to only two offshore rock locations on Santa Catalina. Today this species is beginning to recolonize the island.

WILLIAM W. BUSHING

F. G. HOCHBERG

The malva rosa was once found only on Bird Rock.

DOUG PROPST

TERRY MARTIN

The dusty miller is a coastal bluff resident.

This subspecies of harvest mouse, indigenous to Santa Catalina, is one of only two native mice on the island.

TERRY MARTIN

The Catalina live forever is found only on this island, but is common and widespread on north coastal bluffs.

DOUG PROPST

North-facing ridges are graced by Catalina manzanita.

DOUG PROPST

Only a handful of adult Catalina mahoganies exist in the wild, but recent conservation efforts have vastly increased this species' chances of survival. New seedlings now thrive in protected areas.

Early spring brings a new crop of tawny baby bison. Frisky first-year calves soon grow horns that stand straight out. By the second year these horns will begin to curve upward, and by the third, they will curve in over the animal's head. Older bison frequently show signs of age in broken or blunted tips on their horns. The horns of male bison are larger at the base than their eye-ring.

THE LIVING WEB

Plants provide a matrix and a foundation for the animals of Catalina. The plant life is everything to them, from the smallest native insects to the huge American bison. Most visitors think of bison and goats when they think of Catalina's animals, but the island has many native animals of equal attractiveness and of great biological interest.

Within the camouflage of the grass and brush lies a group of frequently overlooked animals. Insects, though poorly studied, are among the most interesting of Catalina's inhabitants because some of them apparently evolved to survive in the island's unique environmental conditions. Crickets and walking sticks are the most studied insects on the island. Several species are unique to Catalina. Study of other insect groups may yield new species as well, and with them, a chance to gain insight into the processes of evolution and natural selection.

Also of interest are the birds that prey on the insects, because far fewer bird species exist here than on the mainland. The island's isolation has resulted in a relatively small list of all bird species. Among those conspicuously absent are many birds common in mainland yards and gardens, like the scrub jay and the crow. Those that made the

A profusion of gulls are in the water around the island, feeding on fish, crustaceans, and handouts. One species, the western gull, nests on Bird Rock in Isthmus Harbor.

JEFF GNASS

Catalina quail abound in the island's hills. Large coveys are frequently seen parading down the roads in no apparent hurry to yield to traffic.

ROBERT GIVEN

DAVID K. GARCELON

Bald eagles are now a common sight to boating enthusiasts who see these birds on high coastal cliffs scanning the sea for fish.

arduous crossing from the mainland, including the raven, the mockingbird, and the Rufous-sided towhee, are free to exploit resources that were denied to them by competition from other birds on the mainland.

Catalina also has its share of endemic birds. The Catalina quail, a larger and darker subspecies of its mainland relative, is found in its natural state only on Catalina Island. The Bewick's wren is also an endemic, while the loggerhead shrike subspecies is found only on the Channel Islands.

In the past, the Channel Islands and Catalina were home to the bald eagle and the peregrine falcon. A combination of pesticides and human abuse resulted in their extinction in the 1950s. Joint programs involving the Institute for Wildlife Studies, the Peregrine Fund and the Catalina Conservancy have reintroduced both birds to Santa Catalina. Once again bald eagles and peregrine falcons hunt from coastal cliffs. Once again the majestic bald eagle enhances the cliffs and airways of the island. The lessons learned at Catalina will help scientists restore populations on the other Channel Islands.

Reptiles and amphibians have found their way to the island too. Catalina is the only Channel Island with a resident rattlesnake, one of the largest natural predators. Although this animal stirs caution in the minds of hikers, it plays an essential role in controlling rodent populations, keeping the island ecosystem in balance.

Another reptile, the aquatic garter snake, provides a clue to the colonization of the island. This snake is closely related to a garter snake living only in the Santa Ynez River drainage north of Point Conception, above Santa Barbara. The island species probably arrived by rafting, perhaps on a storm-downed oak from the Santa Ynez River.

Why is it that this alligator lizard made it to the island but the mainland's more common western fence lizard did not?

Many of Santa Catalina's terrestrial inhabitants probably arrived in similar ways. Other reptiles include the side-blotched lizard, the alligator lizard, and a skink.

The presence of amphibians on the island is particularly hard to explain. By nature, they are unable to tolerate the desiccating effects of salt water. The very small ones like the Pacific tree frog and the slender salamander are found naturally on Catalina. These probably arrived via rotten tree stumps, like the huge redwood stump that washed ashore at Little Harbor in 1960.

Rarely seen or appreciated are the island's native mammals. Harvest and deer mice are seldom noticed by visitors, except unwary backpackers who frequently meet them as food thieves. Deer mice are a subspecies found only on the island. And very little is known about the island's shrew species, which has been seen only a few times in the last century.

The Catalina subspecies of the Channel Island fox is the largest native mammalian predator on the island. How did it arrive? Was it brought as a pet by the Indians who inhabited the island? Or did it arrive by rafting from the mainland or from another island? No one knows. Distantly related to the mainland gray fox, the island fox is different in several ways. It is small—about the size of a house cat. Its diet consists largely of fruits, berries, and insects. The island fox's most special traits are lack of fear coupled with intense natural curiosity. In fact, a chance encounter between human and fox frequently results in both parties sitting down and studying each other with keen interest for several seconds or even minutes.

The island fox gives an interesting insight into human impacts on the island ecosystem. The friendly fox has suffered at the unwitting hands of people who introduced non-native grasses with the first grazing animals. Hitchhiking wild oat seeds—the kind that stick in hikers' socks— inevitably arrived with the grasses. These seeds get into the fox's eyes, causing blindness. This makes it hard for the fox to find food and leaves it susceptible to attack by another of man's introductions, the feral house cat. The result of these intrusions into the fox's domain is that Catalina probably has the lowest-density fox population of all the Channel Islands.

Alien animals from ants to bison have been introduced to the island. The larger ones add character to the island's rugged hills, but only at considerable cost to native plants and animals. Pigs, introduced to eat rattlesnakes, also eat mice, shrews, and acorns. Moreover, they root in the soil for grubs and bulbs. Consequently the island, once heavily forested, has had little or no reproduction of forest trees. As the trees disappear, habitat for many seldom seen native animals, like the arboreal salamander and ornate shrew, becomes scarcer and they decline too.

The native rattlesnake plays an important role as a predator of rodent populations.

Management of the fragile island ecosystem is difficult and, because of the effects of alien animals, expensive. Fortunately, farsighted managers started programs many years ago that enable return of much of the island to its natural state. Those parts of the island will be a kind of laboratory not found at colleges and universities—a natural laboratory for the study of evolution and ecology, a rare commodity worthy of protection.

SUGGESTED READING

CARLQUIST, SHERWIN J. *Island Biology.* New York: Columbia University Press, 1974.

HOWORTH, PETER C. *Channel Islands: The Story Behind the Scenery.* Las Vegas, Nevada: KC Publications, 1982.

MUNZ, PHILIP A. *A Flora of Southern California.* Berkeley: University of California Press, 1974.

POWER, DENNIS M., ed. *The California Islands: Proceedings of a Multidisciplinary Symposium.* Santa Barbara, California: Santa Barbara Museum of Natural History, 1980.

STEPHEN BENNETT

Early morning and late evening are the best times to spot the inquisitive Channel Island fox.

In the past, uncontrolled herds of feral goats did extensive damage to Catalina's vegetation. Over 40 species of plants have vanished. Terraced and eroded hillsides are reminders of the damage once done. Green hills, new seedlings, spring wildflowers, and clear streams are the rewards of years of careful management.

DAVID K. GARCELON

Overleaf: New winter oak leaves await spring warmth and moisture. Photo by Jeff Gnass.

Where the Currents Meet

At Catalina the cold, nutrient-rich waters of the California Current mix with warm southern waters in what is called a transitional zone. A great diversity of habitats occurs in this zone, from exposed coast to protected mud flats. The combination of temperatures, habitats, and abundant food results in dense and diverse plant and animal life, revealed in water that is often quite clear. Shells and storm-tossed kelp litter sandy beaches and rocky coves, a reminder that life abounds in the shallow waters nearby. Some forms, like sea urchins, lobsters, and abalones, are of commercial importance.

The shallow mud flats at Ballast Point, within the protected waters of Catalina Harbor, support the only Channel Island population of the entertaining fiddler crab. Children and adults can sit entranced, watching the scurrying antics of this mud-flat dweller as it searches out food and postures in defense, its one giant and one diminutive claw held out like shield and sword.

Also found on the mud flats is a curious plant known as eelgrass. This is a true flowering plant, but it is specially adapted for living underwater. Male flowers release pollen grains consisting of long filaments of the same density as seawater. The pollen is carried by currents to a female flower, where it has a good chance of adhering to the stigma, thus pollinating the plant.

Eelgrass meadows, as well as surfgrass areas and kelp beds, are important spawning and feeding areas for fin fishes. The garibaldi is one of the most colorful of the kelp-bed fish; it looks like an overgrown goldfish. Uncontrolled harvesting of

Deserted beaches await those who take the time and effort to explore the island. But watch the tide. Some beaches are high and dry during low tide and completely underwater once the tide comes in.

JEFF GNASS

The garibaldi is often the first marine fish a visitor to Catalina meets. The bright hue of the fish allows it to be easily seen through the clear water from a cruise boat. Protected by law, this colorful creature was once overfished, greatly reducing their numbers. The male prepares and guards the nest.

THOMAS COWELL

the garibaldi in earlier times decreased its numbers, forcing California to declare it a protected species.

An excellent place to meet shallow-water sea creatures is at Lover's Cove. Here, people can peer from glass-bottomed boats or snorkel along the surface, observing fish mingled in a beautiful array of colors against the background of an algal rock garden. Kelp bass, opaleye, and garibaldi jostle to accept bread-crumb handouts from excited divers.

Where small fish abound, larger fish are always close by. Skates and rays occasionally thrill the snorkelers. The horned shark is an inshore species whose egg case resembles a large screw, possibly an adaptation for holding the capsule in place in the rocks until it hatches. Visitors frequently find egg cases, commonly called mermaid purses, thrown up on the beach by the sea. While most egg cases are empty, one held up to the sun sometimes reveals a living embryo within. Prompt return to the ocean may help it survive.

The deeper waters offshore have long been known for their game fish. Marlin and tuna attract many sport fishermen each year. Large sharks prowl offshore too, and some are feisty game fish in their own right. These deeper waters also sup-

WILLIAM W. BUSHING

Glass bottom boats provide visitors who don't want to get wet with a close-up view of the marine life.

Brown pelicans feed by day. Some seek safe island roost sites at nightfall.

WILLIAM W. BUSHING

port a hardy band of commercial fishermen and fleets of charter boats filled with sport fishermen trying their luck.

Anyone who has ever fished off the island is well aware of the large numbers of seabirds found offshore. Although gulls and brown pelicans normally feed on anchovies and other small marine life, they have learned to augment their diet with handouts and outright thefts from fishermen. Frequently the results of such behavior are fishhooks embedded in their throat and monofilament line wrapped around their wings.

Many birds seen over the water by day roost or breed along the precipitous headlands and rugged, inaccessible rocky shores where good feeding sites are found close by. Catalina is a fine place to watch for both resident and migrant birds. For some species it is an important nesting habitat.

There are several species of cetaceans—whales, dolphins, and porpoises—that can be found off Catalina. Some, like the pilot whale, may breed in areas like Ironbound Cove. Pinnipeds—seals and sea lions—frequently crawl out of the water to rest on rocks and beaches. Califor-

Harbor seals seem to adapt well to humans in their underwater realm. Dozens of these beautiful creatures may be born on the island's peaceful beaches each spring.

THOMAS COWELL

Under the right conditions, forests of giant kelp can grow as much as two feet a day. Scientists are studying ways to use this resource to provide future energy sources.

LOUIS PREZELIN

nia sea lions visit the island yearly. In spring as many as 350 of these sleek creatures may be seen sunning themselves on rocks near the eastern tip of the island. Many a diver has had the thrill of playing hide-and-seek in the kelp beds with the puppy-faced, curious harbor seal. A few lucky individuals have stumbled across a baby harbor seal on the beach, apparently abandoned, but in reality only left alone while its mother is fishing nearby. About 100 harbor seals breed on secluded beaches each year.

One marine mammal not seen in the last century around Catalina is the sea otter. Pelt hunters eliminated the otter from these waters in the 1800s. We can learn some lessons in ecosystem management from the otter's passing, for with the decline of the otter came an increase in sea urchins and other invertebrates that the otter ate. Sea urchin populations boomed, so the sea urchin's food—kelp—decreased. Fish and other creatures that lived and bred in kelp forests probably declined as well. This is but one example of the tradeoffs involved in modifying an ecosystem. Humans should exercise care in alteration of ecosystems because the effects of their actions are not always immediately apparent or predictable.

Several areas around the island provide habitats for some unusual plants and animals. The waters around the western third of the island are a transitional zone for species with northern and southern affinities. The east end contains a subtidal sand habitat where the orange-throat pike blenny lives. This small fish is found only in a few places off the Channel Islands and in the Gulf of California. Offshore, Farnsworth Bank, a series of rock pinnacles rising to within 50 feet of the surface, has been set aside as an ecological reserve to protect the rare purple coral.

With so much unusual marine life, you would expect that scientists would flock to Catalina to study it. In fact, they do come to the University of Southern California's Marine Science Center, located at Big Fisherman's Cove. This center,

These pelagic red crabs are an unexpected bounty for the island's gulls. The crabs accompany the El Niño current, a surge of warm tropical water that strikes California every few years.

JEFF GNASS

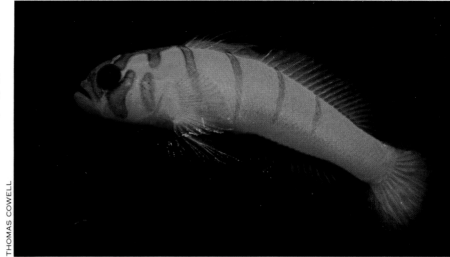

Bright colors adorn this goby, providing a visual reward to divers exploring California's depths.

THOMAS COWELL

The orange-throat pike blenny is representative of the transitional zone found in the waters off Santa Catalina. The Channel Island waters mark the northernmost range of this fish.

THOMAS COWELL

HENRY GENTHE

Farnsworth Bank, only a few miles off Catalina, is the home of this purple coral.

through the Institute for Marine and Coastal Studies, supports education and research in marine science, engineering, and policy. A hyperbaric chamber used in medical and biological research is housed here. Victims of diving accidents, including the "bends," or decompression sickness, are brought here from all over southern California. Many divers owe their life to this facility.

Over the years the island's waters have changed because of human use. Old-timers remember when the sea life was much more abundant; when fishing and diving were more productive. Visitors must now treat the ocean's waters, the sea floor, and the beaches with care. Obeying the rules will ensure that the marine resources continue to be productive for future generations.

SUGGESTED READING

FAGAN, BRIAN. *A Cruising Guide to California's Channel Islands.* Ventura, California: Western Marine Enterprises, 1983.

HINTON, SAM. *Seashore Life of Southern California.* California National History Guide, No. 26. Berkeley: University of California Press, 1969.

HOWORTH, PETER. *Foraging Along the California Coast.* Santa Barbara, California: Capra Press, 1977.

Those Who Came Before...

With such an abundance of marine life, it was natural that early man would exploit that bounty. Some parts of the island were inhabited by ancient cultures as much as 6,800 years ago. The earliest evidence of human habitation was discovered in the Little Harbor area on the island's southwest shore. This evidence consisted of charcoal found in midden sites—trash dumps—left by those people. Radiocarbon dating techniques used on this material established these estimates. Little is known about these earliest inhabitants, but they were probably hunters and gatherers who fished the island's waters and harvested the rich intertidal resources.

More is known about the most recent native inhabitants, the Gabrielino. This knowledge is based on archaeological evidence and early written accounts. Even so, descriptions of these people are speculative and largely based on assumed similarities with coastal peoples.

Most archaeologists believe that the Channel Island and coastal inhabitants shared a similar culture centered upon the Pacific Ocean's resources. This varied between tribes due to environmental and geographical factors rather than because of differences in tribal structure or language. Still, little is certain about the Gabrielino cultural structure. Much archaeological work remains to be done on Catalina, so the beliefs of today will have to be re-examined in the light of future research.

The ancestors of Catalina's Gabrielino originated on the Great Plains and spoke a Shoshonean dialect. The people we call the Gabrielino arrived in southern California about 500 B.C. They wedged their way between the Hokan-speaking tribes who originally inhabited the area, pushing them north and south. The Gabrielino constituted a division of the Canalino culture found both on the coast and on the Channel Islands. The natives

DOUG PROPST

The only way to learn about the original inhabitants of Catalina is by scientific investigation of archaeological sites. Despite the ravaging of many of these sites by "pot hunters" in times past, a surprising amount of information can still be gleaned from bone and tool fragments, stone bowl remains, and even from seeds and shells found in middens (ancient refuse heaps).

Cactus and oak provided the earliest inhabitants with food resources that supplemented the sea's bounty.

JEFF GNASS

JEFF GNASS

of Catalina called themselves *Pimugnans,* for they called their island *Pima* or *Pimugna.* This culture was crystalized by A.D. 1000, to endure until the arrival of the Spaniards some 500 years later. By then the culture was far removed from its Shoshonean heritage. Like other coastal tribes, the culture was based upon the sea and trade.

At Avalon, the Isthmus, and Little Harbor, on the southwest shore, were major village sites, each occupied by possibly 500 people. Some 40 smaller village sites were scattered around the island near permanent sources of water, while literally thousands of smaller sites existed. As many as 500 to 2,500 Pimugnans may have lived on the island at one time.

Abundant intertidal marine life is concealed by a rich blanket of seaweed. This is a legacy left in few places in southern California. When you realize how much the sea can actually provide, it is easy to imagine how the island could support more than 2,000 native people.

Lodgings were domed structures constructed of a willow framework covered with tule thatching. Each structure housed several families. Larger villages were governed by a chief and a *shaman*, or medicine man. The shaman was also a priest of the distinctive Gabrielino religion called *Chinigchinich* which gave rules that governed each individual's life. Rattlesnakes and ravens were given godlike importance, which may account for the raven's bold behavior around humans today.

The needs of the islanders were readily obtained by what some early descriptions call "the graceful, easy style" of the native fishermen. They threw bone harpoons attached to lines to catch large fish and marine mammals. The people also gathered intertidal shellfish, which probably provided a large part of their diet. Evidence indicates that part of this food was smoked for a reserve or possibly for trade. Their diet was rounded out with bulbs from the relatives of the wild onion and roots of the wild cucumber, along with prickly pears and acorns harvested from the large oak forests. What little clothing was needed was fashioned from the natural materials available, including otter furs and marine bird feathers ornamented with shell beads and stones. The Gabrielino were skilled and handsome people.

The most important advance in Gabrielino culture was the art of soapstone carving. Soapstone is impure steatite, a talc-schist, metamorphic rock found in outcrops. Soapstone is very soft, which makes it easy to carve and polish. This material was widely used in making figurines and *ollas* (OY-yahs)—natural crockpots of sorts. The ollas were used in cooking because their high talc content made them relatively immune to heat fracture, a common problem with other types of stone bowls.

Olla manufacture comprised an uncomplicated process of finding a soapstone outcrop, carving out a bowl blank, then gradually refining it to finished proportions. To accomplish this, tools including slate saws, quartz gouges, grinding stones, and polishing materials were used. Soapstone outcrops still showing bowl scars and quarry pits are common, especially near some of the high peaks in the interior. Fragments of bowls litter

JEFF GNASS

Steatite, or soapstone, is a product of the island's geologic past. The Gabrielino quarried it out and turned it to good use as ollas, or stone crockpots, that were the basis of an extensive trade with the mainland.

hillsides below some of these sites. You can almost hear the curses of a frustrated bowl carver as he hurled the fragments down the hill after a bowl broke in his hands.

The easily made, useful ollas were in great demand on the mainland in places where soapstone was absent. A flourishing trade developed, accomplished by a journey across the 20-mile San Pedro Channel in open, planked canoes called *tiats*. The channel crossings may have taken less than four hours under favorable conditions—truly remarkable time. The Gabrielino also traded with native of the other islands. In fact, the design of their watercraft was possibly borrowed from the Chumash Indians inhabiting the islands and mainland to the north.

Through research it has become evident that Santa Catalina's natives adapted to their environ-

Catalina may have looked like this when Cabrillo first set foot on the island. His party may have put ashore near White's Landing, in the left foreground, at a place now called Cabrillo Beach. How much the island has changed since his arrival we can only guess.

DOUG PROPST

A lack of abundant fresh water deterred Spaniards from establishing a mission here. But year-round streams like this one in Middle Canyon provide water today for over 2,000 residents and countless visitors.

WILLIAM W. BUSHING

ment in many ways. They exploited many types of marine and terrestrial resources and developed specialized ways of processing food. Their quarrying operations were extensive. They modified their environment too, by harvesting acorns and bulbs and quite possibly by introducing new species of plants and animals. In all, they formed a vigorous, flourishing culture actively linked with other cultures through trade.

The Catalina Island of today is much different from the way it was when the Gabrielino lived here. The roots and acorns on which they lived are now far less abundant. The marine resources are not as bountiful as they once were. Far fewer seabirds and mammals visit the island. The story of the Pimugnan's decline is not one of environmental change, but that of the ravages of European disease and the effects of the fierce otter hunters.

EUROPEANS ARRIVE

At dawn on October 7, 1542, the first Europeans landed on Catalina, probably at the broad protected beach of what is now White's Landing. Juan Rodriguez Cabrillo, a Portuguese navigator sailing for the Spanish crown, named the island San Salvador and claimed it for Spain. The explorers were greeted warmly by the Pimugnan. Soon the natives incorporated Spanish metal tools into their soapstone manufacturing process.

In 1602, Sebastián Vizcaíno arrived at what he thought was an undiscovered island and renamed it Santa Catalina in honor of that saint's impending feast day. In all, Catalina's entry into the Spanish empire had little effect on the island and aroused little outside interest until the mission period.

Spanish mission fathers may have seen Catalina's pagan natives as a threat to the successful conversion of mainland peoples. Although the priests wanted to build a mission there, a measles epidemic occurred in 1805 that wiped out some 200 Indians. This tragedy, combined with a lack of water and farmland and dwindling government support, doomed the mission fathers' goal.

The thriving sea-otter trade attracted to the island fierce Aleut hunters on Russian ships. The priests, fearing for the Indians' safety, may have removed many of them to the missions. The records substantiate only a few arrivals at the San Gabriel Mission—hence the name, Gabrielino—as well as at other missions. Between social disruption and disease, probably no Native Americans inhabited the island by the end of the mission period in 1832.

High tariffs were placed on imported goods in the early 1800s by the Spanish government. Catalina played an important role in undermining those trade restrictions. Yankee traders, who dominated west coast trade, would stop at the island and unload large portions of their trade goods, then proceed to the mainland to pay customs duties on their reduced cargo. With duties paid, they returned to the island, picked up the remainder of their goods and sold them duty-free up the coast. Other traders visited the island to store goods or to use fine ports like Avalon in which to repair their vessels.

Catalina's use by traders and smugglers as a place to store cargo and avoid customs duties has continued until recent times. It was also used as a layover for smuggled Chinese laborers until the late 1800s, and as a transfer point for illicit prohibition and drugs in the twentieth century.

Few facts are known about the pioneer settlers who came to the island after the demise of the Indians. For 14 years the island was occupied by squatters who made a living at ranching with stock they had brought to the island or possibly with animals that had escaped from early smugglers or missionaries.

One of the best known of the squatters was Samuel Prentiss, who made his living by fishing, hunting, and selling firewood. Legend states that he had originally come to the island to search for rumored Indian and smuggled treasure, which he never found. Prentiss died in 1854. For years a marker identified his grave on the windy cliffs above the sea.

An otter hunter who played an important role in the island's history was George Yount, who searched for gold here in 1830. Yount's quest for a bonanza brought him back to the island several times but without success.

JEFF GNASS

The rugged canyons on the island's windward slope are long and in many areas are fringed by steep hills. Within these canyons streams run over bedrock outcrops year round.

Squatters and smugglers dominated the island in the declining years of Mexican rule. The war between the United States and Mexico profoundly changed the island's history. In 1846, the last Mexican governor of Alta California, Pío Pico, allegedly gave title to Catalina to Thomas Robbins of Santa Barbara in exchange for a saddle and a fresh horse. Pico was fleeing from advancing American troops at the time. Robbins brought a degree of order to ranching on Catalina, and by the early 1860s as many as 60 head of cattle, 8,000 goats, 20,000 sheep and other assorted livestock grazed here.

Through a period of title transfers, the lure of gold still brought miners, culminating in a "gold rush" centered on the Isthmus. In January of 1864, the U.S. Army established a garrison at the Isthmus, which cooled the gold fever. Their old barracks building is now the home of the Isthmus Yacht Club. Even though lead, silver, and zinc were discovered on the island, most of the settlers had returned to ranching by 1868.

George Shatto purchased Catalina in 1887. He was the first to cater to the tourist trade by renting tent spaces to vacationers on the flats above Avalon Bay. Later a stage road designed by Samuel Farnsworth was completed. Many parts of this road are still in use today. The road allowed limited development of tourist facilities at Little Harbor, Emerald Bay, and Eagle's Nest. This trend toward development and tourism continued with the 1892 purchase of the financially troubled island by the Banning brothers, who founded the Santa Catalina Island Company shortly thereafter.

Financial difficulties continued for the island's owners until 1919 when a majority interest was purchased by William Wrigley Jr., chewing-gum magnate. This was followed shortly by Wrigley's acquisition of complete title to the island company. With Wrigley and his heirs came a new era for the island. Although tourism continued to be important, appreciation of the island's unique resources and historical importance grew, leading the way to a tradition of conservation and careful management. This heritage enables preservation of the beauty, natural diversity, and charm of Santa Catalina for all its future visitors.

Early visitors to the island found Avalon's sheltered bay, clear water, and gentle shoreline extremely attractive. These travelers bragged about the fishing, marveled at the seals and sea lions, and enjoyed coach tours of the interior. As a result, Avalon developed into a tourist haven even before the turn of the century. Careful comparison of this picture with the front cover will show some remarkable differences. Sugar Loaf Peak has been replaced by the Casino, the cobble beach is now covered with imported sand, and the vegetation on the hillsides appears healthier today.

Avalon in 1886—

Reyes Photo

William Wrigley, Jr., and Phillip K. Wrigley were largely responsible for the development of Avalon. Their love of the island established a tradition of careful management that has saved this special place for all to enjoy and appreciate.

COURTESY SANTA CATALINA ISLAND COMPANY

JEFF GNASS

SUGGESTED READING

ANGLE, PAUL M. *Philip K. Wrigley: A Memoir of a Modest Man*. Chicago: Rand McNally Co., 1975.

DORAN, ADELAIDE L. *The Ranch that was Robbins': Santa Catalina Island, California; A Source Book*. Glendale: Arthur H. Clark Co., 1963.

GREGG, A. L. "A History of Santa Catalina Island from 1542–1919." Master's thesis, University of Southern California, 1934.

JOHNSTON, BERNICE E. *California's Gabrielino Indians*. Los Angeles: Southwest Museum, 1962.

WINDLE, ERNEST. *Windle's History of Santa Catalina Island*. 2nd ed. Avalon, California: The Catalina Islander, 1940.

Old Eagle's Nest Stagecoach Stop is a remnant of the development of island tourism. The lodge is almost unchanged from the way it looked in the 1800s.

Avalon

WILLIAM W. BUSHING

Catalina tile, today prized by collectors for its superb workmanship and rarity, was once a major island industry.

JEFF GNASS

Pleasantly nestled among the steep hills of Avalon Canyon lies the city of Avalon, the waterfront population center of Catalina. A pleasant anchorage for boating enthusiasts, an escape for city dwellers, a shopping and dining paradise, Avalon offers a great deal. Summer crowds color the beaches with tanned skin and bright swimwear while all manner of yachts fill the bay. Winter visitors find pleasant weather and restful quiet amid hills teeming with flowers. Avalon also caters to the most cultivated tastes. Concerts, dances, and theatre enrich the nightlife. Business people find a conference here a welcome departure from the metropolitan bustle of the mainland. A quick call to the Catalina Chamber of Commerce will provide up-to-date information on all the latest events. The island visitor center helps guests plan details of their stay. The residents are friendly, the pace, relaxed.

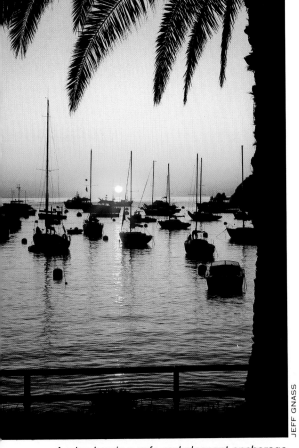

Avalon bay is a safe and pleasant anchorage.

The "front street," lined with shops, hotels, and restaurants, faces the beach and bay.

Waterfront dining awaits the visitor who can't bear to leave the beach.

This golfers' green was a beach in prehistoric times.

The impressive Wrigley Memorial was built almost entirely of native materials, while the exotic plants nearby came from every corner of the earth. The Wrigley Memorial Garden Foundation, supported by members, maintains this beautiful place.

Avalon

Today's Catalina is an attractive blend of wilderness and resort. The Wrigley Garden in upper Avalon Canyon embodies this unusual blend. Here, exotic plants and island endemics are intertwined in attractive plantings along the meandering paths. But the garden is more than a thing of beauty; it is also a place where important research on California's flora is carried out.

Avalon itself is named after a mythical island valley in a Tennyson poem ". . . where falls not hail or rain, or any snow, nor ever wind blows loudly; but it lies deep-meadowed, happy, fair with orchard lawns and bowery hallows crown'd with summer seas . . ." The reality of the city of Avalon is almost as good as Tennyson's description. The safe harbor, fine hotels, and superb restaurants make this one of the finest resort destinations in America. Each year Avalon attracts many thousands of people.

Visitors are treated to a variety of experiences. They can choose from bustling nightlife to an early-morning run along deserted streets. The flavor of Avalon changes with the seasons. In summer the beaches teem with sunbathers while yacht parties prevail and happy crowds stroll the streets. During winter the crisp, clean feel of rain-washed skies pervades, and the atmosphere is quiet and relaxed.

WILLIAM W. BUSHING

Avalon's renowned beaches and warm waters attract many visitors.

Inland bus tours provide an easy armchair view of the island's interior. The drivers provide a practiced commentary en route.

COURTESY SANTA CATALINA ISLAND COMPANY

43

Two Harbors has provided the set for many a Hollywood movie including "Mutiny on the Bounty" and "Hurricane." It is still used in film productions. Many a Hollywood star has found the Isthmus a pleasant place to retreat from the rush of film life.

JEFF GNASS

Two Harbors

Two Harbors, located between Catalina and Isthmus harbors, is a popular destination for yachting aficionados looking for a different experience than that found at Avalon. Only one restaurant, a store, and a hunting lodge exist here for entertainment, but they are every bit as good as Avalon's best. In addition to boating, hiking and diving adventures are available to visitors at this quiet but wild part of the island.

Sailing enthusiasts enjoy fair afternoon winds and moderate swells off the island's north shore.

THOMAS COWELL

Roughing it at Parson's Landing is fun for hardy families.

JASON RUBINSTEEN

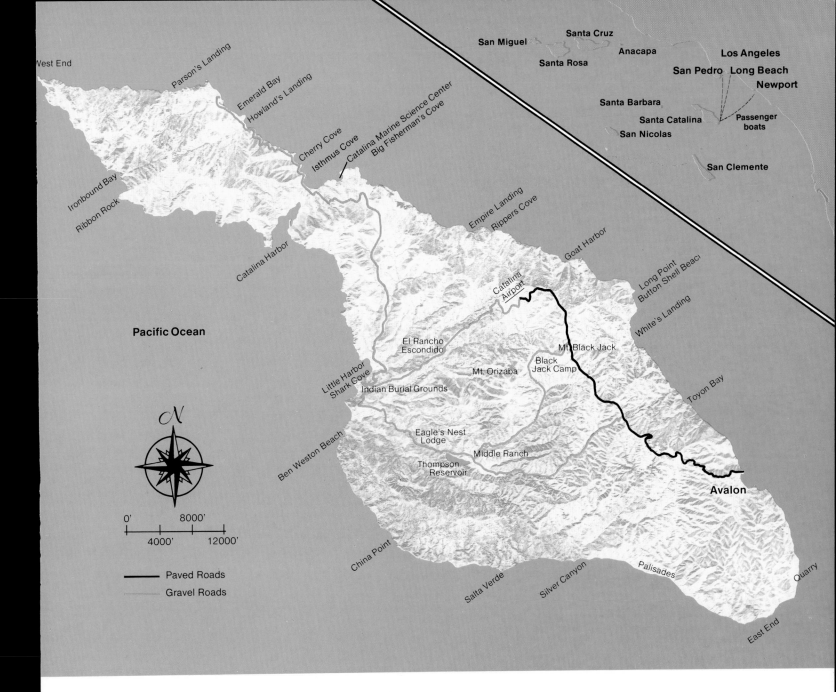

West End

Parson's Landing

Emerald Bay

Howland's Landing

Cherry Cove

Isthmus Cove

Catalina Marine Science Center

Big Fisherman's Cove

Ironbound Bay

Ribbon Rock

Catalina Harbor

Empire Landing

Rippers Cove

Goat Harbor

Long Point

Button Shell Beach

White's Landing

Pacific Ocean

Catalina Airport

El Rancho Escondido

Mt Black Jack

Black Jack Camp

Mt. Orizaba

Little Harbor

Shark Cove

Indian Burial Grounds

Toyon Bay

Eagle's Nest Lodge

Middle Ranch

Ben Weston Beach

Thompson Reservoir

Avalon

China Point

Salta Verde

Silver Canyon

Palisades

Quarry

East End

San Miguel

Santa Cruz

Santa Rosa

Anacapa

Los Angeles

San Pedro Long Beach

Newport

Santa Barbara

Santa Catalina

Passenger boats

San Nicolas

San Clemente

0'   8000'
4000'   12000'

——— Paved Roads
——— Gravel Roads

TERRY MARTIN

The Isthmus, a narrow neck of land, connects the rugged west end of the island to the larger eastern two-thirds of Santa Catalina. Only 30 feet above sea level and half a mile wide, the Isthmus apparently fooled Juan Rodriquez Cabrillo into thinking that this was two separate islands in 1542.

Overleaf: The Summit Road winds through the hills above Avalon. Photo by Jeff Gnass

The Island Tomorrow

The Santa Catalina Island Conservancy, a private nonprofit membership foundation, was formed in 1972 to preserve the natural resources of the island. In 1974, the Santa Catalina Island Company guaranteed public access to the island by granting an open-space easement to Los Angeles County. The following year title to 86 percent of the island was passed to the Conservancy. Since 1975 this organization has become responsible for the interior roads, beaches, and even the Airport-in-the-Sky, perched 1,600 feet above the sea. The Conservancy strives to encourage appreciation of the island through careful management, education, conservation, and research. In carrying out these aims, they work closely with other agencies having similar goals.

As part of its expanding program, the Catalina Conservancy now conducts a range of educational activities including slide shows, nature hikes, and natural history programs at the newly constructed Nature Center and at other island and mainland locations. These projects help explain the unique features of the island to visitors from all walks of life and of all ages. The Conservancy also assists researchers and student interns with their projects. Ongoing programs feature volunteer activities that stress conservation and at the same time work to restore and protect endangered parts of the island ecosystem. The work of the Catalina Conservancy has made Santa Catalina Island a living symbol of people's willingness to help preserve our natural heritage.

The Catalina Conservancy offers island appreciation walks for visitors who want an intimate insight into the island's natural resources.

DOUG PROPST

Books on National Park areas in "The Story Behind the Scenery" series are: Acadia, Alcatraz Island, Arches, Badlands, Big Bend, Biscayne, Blue Ridge Parkway, Bryce Canyon, Canyon de Chelly, Canyonlands, Cape Cod, Capitol Reef, Channel Islands, Civil War Parks, Colonial, Crater Lake, Death Valley, Denali, Devils Tower, Dinosaur, Everglades, Fort Clatsop, Gettysburg, Glacier, Glen Canyon-Lake Powell, Grand Canyon, Grand Canyon-North Rim, Grand Teton, Great Basin, Great Smoky Mountains, Haleakalā, Hawai`i Volcanoes, Independence, Joshua Tree, Lake Mead-Hoover Dam, Lassen Volcanic, Lincoln Parks, Mammoth Cave, Mesa Verde, Mount Rainier, Mount Rushmore, Mount St. Helens, National Park Service, National Seashores, North Cascades, Olympic, Petrified Forest, Redwood, Rocky Mountain, Scotty's Castle, Sequoia & Kings Canyon, Shenandoah, Statue of Liberty, Theodore Roosevelt, Virgin Islands, Yellowstone, Yosemite, Zion.

Additional books in "The Story Behind the Scenery" series are: Annapolis, Big Sur, California Gold Country, California Trail, Colorado Plateau, Columbia River Gorge, Fire: A Force of Nature, Grand Circle Adventure, John Wesley Powell, Kauai, Lake Tahoe, Las Vegas, Lewis & Clark, Monument Valley, Mormon Temple Square, Mormon Trail, Mount St. Helens, Nevada's Red Rock Canyon, Nevada's Valley of Fire, Oregon Trail, Oregon Trail Center, Santa Catalina, Santa Fe Trail, Sharks, Sonoran Desert, U.S. Virgin Islands, Water: A Gift of Nature, Whales.

Call (800-626-9673), fax (702-433-3420), or write to the address below.

Published by KC Publications, 3245 E. Patrick Ln., Suite A, Las Vegas, NV 89120.

The Casino overlooks sleeping Avalon Harbor. The bustle of Los Angeles is lost across the channel. Photo by Jeff Gnass.

Created, Designed, and Published in the U.S.A.
Printed by Doosan Dong-A Co., Ltd., Seoul, Korea
Color Separations by Kedia/Kwang Yang Sa Co., Ltd.
Paper produced exclusively by Hankuk Paper Mfg. Co., Ltd.